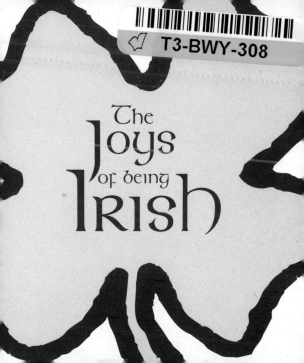

The
Joys
of being
Irish

The Joys of being Irish

Terrance McDevitt

**Andrews McMeel
Publishing**

Kansas City

The Joys of Being Irish

ISBN: 0-7407-2204-2

Library of Congress Catalog Card Number: 2002102328

03 04 05 06 07 BID 10 9 8 7 6 5 4 3 2 1

Attention: Schools and Businesses

Andrews McMeel books are available at quantity dis-
counts with bulk purchase for educational, business, or
sales promotional use. For information, please write to:
Special Sales Department, Andrews McMeel Publishing,
4520 Main Street, Kansas City, Missouri 64111.

Introduction

O nce upon a time, you'd see storefront help-wanted signs reading "Irish Need Not Apply." Back then, we were only good enough for the more menial of societal tasks. But that was fine for a culture of survivors. If the Famine didn't kill us, a little ditch digging wouldn't either. And so our grandparents and our great-grandparents struggled and fought and finally flourished in their new land, and now it's other nationalities applying *to be* Irish: Sure, there are hundreds of thousands of Irish-Americans in New York, but not as many as turn out for the St. Patrick's Day Parade.

Of course, there is so much more to being an Irish-American than that over-the-top orgy of green beer and paper shamrocks. But having built so much of America, the Irish somewhere along the way tore down a lot of their own culture. That doesn't mean it doesn't exist. It's just that we haven't paid enough attention to it. We don't celebrate the musicians and actors and writers and family ties as much as we should. We don't hold in high enough esteem our heritage of poets and farmers and pub life. Um, hold on, scratch that. Maybe we hold pub life in a little *too* high esteem, but you get the picture.

At any rate, this little book is a celebration of that culture. It contains reminiscences, common memories, and stereotypes, of course (some deserved, others not so), that we all share. It is an everyman's (and woman's) history of a nation of immigrant survivors. And by talking about it, arguing about it, and adding your own memories, I hope you'll help that history survive, too. Read it in good health, which is best achieved, page 50 says, by quaffing a wee taste of the dark stuff. So drink up and turn the page! Sláinte!

Claiming the land of saints and scholars as your own.

Possessing of the touch of a poet, a bit of the blarney, and the luck of the Irish.

Knowing that St. Patrick
wasn't really Irish—
that he *chose* to save Ireland.

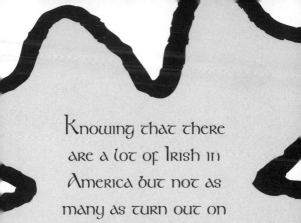

Knowing that there are a lot of Irish in America but not as many as turn out on St. Patrick's Day.

Knowing that those non-Irish
chose Ireland, too.

Celebrating St. Patrick's Day
as they did in the Old Country—
by going to mass.

Knowing that you won't have to go to school on St. Patrick's Day because your mother told the nuns that if it weren't for St. Patrick, you wouldn't be Catholic.

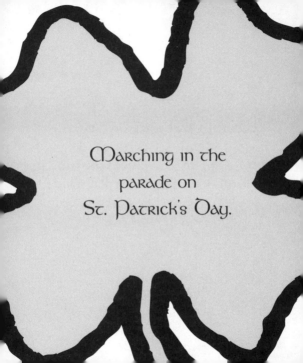

Marching in the
parade on
St. Patrick's Day.

Being forced to
wear green on St. Patrick's Day.

Being forced to wear the hot, itchy,
too-tight Aran sweater that your
Aunt Maggie brought back from
Ireland on St. Patrick's Day.

Being embarrassed that your father is wearing that thirty-year-old hideous green tie on St. Patrick's Day.

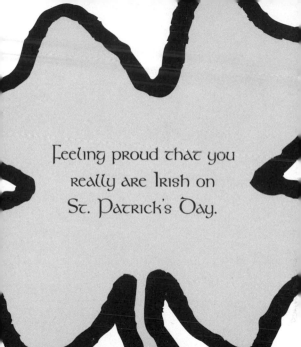

Feeling proud that you
really are Irish on
St. Patrick's Day.

Being able to spot the
wanna-be Irish
on St. Patrick's Day.

Drinking warm green beer
when you were fourteen years old
on St. Patrick's Day.

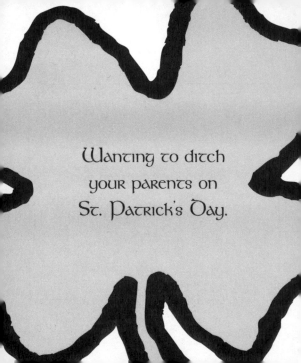

Wanting to ditch
your parents on
St. Patrick's Day.

Hating corned beef and cabbage on
St. Patrick's Day.

Hearing Grandad say there was
no corned beef in Ireland.

Eating Granny's bacon and cabbage
on St. Patrick's Day.

Knowing that it's St. Paddy's Day,
not St. Patty's Day.

As an adult, calling in sick to work
on St. Patrick's Day.

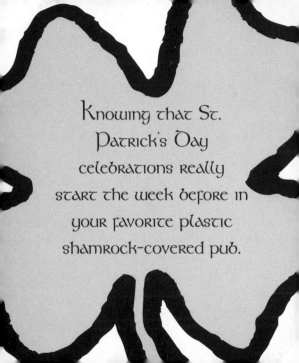

Knowing that St.
Patrick's Day
celebrations really
start the week before in
your favorite plastic
shamrock-covered pub.

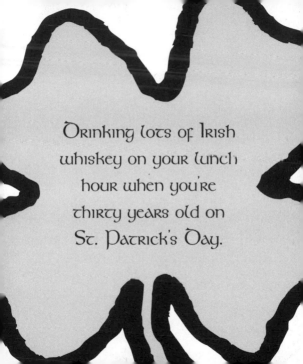

Drinking lots of Irish whiskey on your lunch hour when you're thirty years old on St. Patrick's Day.

Not returning to work after lunch
on St. Patrick's Day.

Wishing that you hadn't been born
Irish the morning after St. Patrick's Day.

Having five older siblings–
and five younger siblings.

Being able to easily remember all your
sisters' names: Mary Kate, Mary Fran,
Mary Beth . . .

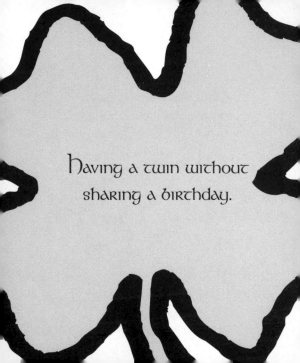

Having a twin without

sharing a birthday.

Having a priest in the family
on call 24/7.

Getting a third name
when you're confirmed.

Claddagh rings.

Aran sweaters.

Donegal tweed.

Belfast linen.

Waterford, Galway,
and Tyrone crystal.

Belleek and Tara china.

Tara china.

Ordering all the above from QVC's annual St. Patrick's Day forty-eight-hour shopping marathon.

Four-leaf clovers.

Limericks.

Irish coffee.

Irish wakes.

Not crying at the wake,
but needing to wipe away the
tears whenever you hear
"Danny Boy."

having enough cousins to field
two football teams.

Seeing all of them only at
wakes and weddings.

Unwrapping a copy of *Brace Yourself Bridget!* at your bridal shower, and discovering that *The Official Irish Sex Manual* is only a few pages long and all of them are blank.

Attending weddings where bagpipers lead the bride up the aisle.

Attending funerals where the bagpipers play at the cemetery.

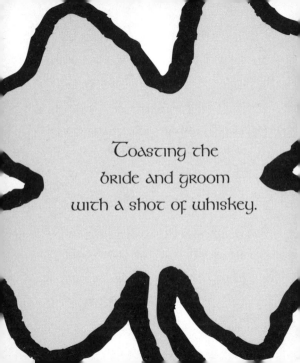

Toasting the
bride and groom
with a shot of whiskey.

Toasting the deceased
with a shot of whiskey.

Toasting too much and fighting with
all your siblings at the wakes.

Toasting too much and fighting with
them at the weddings.

Laying claim to the easiest holiday recipe ever: Place corned beef, cabbage, and potatoes in large pot filled with water. Boil. Eat.

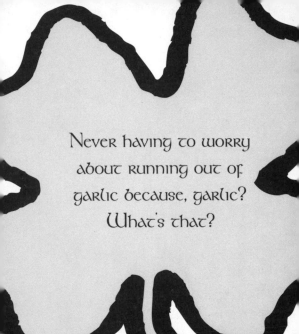

Never having to worry
about running out of
garlic because, garlic?
What's that?

Table salt—the only spice
you'll ever need.

Having a genetic excuse for
alarmingly high cholesterol.

Soda bread.

Knowing that "baking a cake" means making soda bread.

Nearly choking to death
on Granny's dry soda bread
when you were young.

Craving her soda bread as an adult—
but only with plenty of butter and jam.

Potato bread.

Boiled potatoes.

Mashed potatoes.

Fried potatoes.

Spuds any which way.

Knowing that tatties and praties
are spuds, too.

Colcannon.

Such breakfast delicacies as bangers,
rashers, fried bread, and porridge.

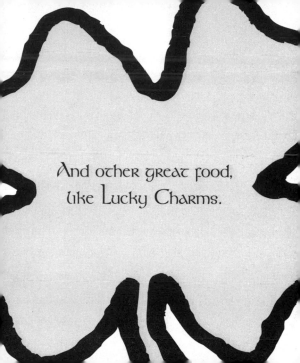

And other great food,
like Lucky Charms.

Knowing that when measured against Irish cuisine, the Famine might not have been all that bad.

Admitting that we don't do so good with food, but no one understands beverages better.

If you're Protestant, only drinking that Catholic whiskey Jameson if the only other choice is vodka.

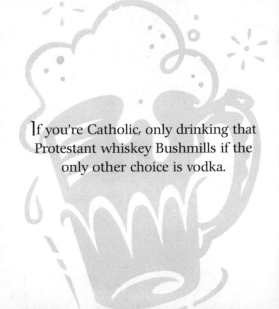

If you're Catholic, only drinking that Protestant whiskey Bushmills if the only other choice is vodka.

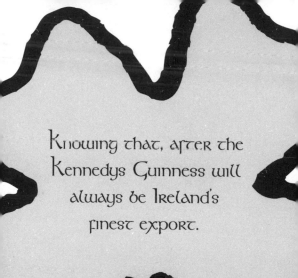

Knowing that, after the Kennedys Guinness will always be Ireland's finest export.

Needing a wee taste of the dark stuff every now and again.

Knowing that Guinness is food.
(There's ate and there's drink in it!)
Even when it's not in that stew.

Believing that Guinness is good for you. (A Guinness a day keeps the doctor away.)

Believing that Guinness will improve your manliness. (Guinness makes you strong.)

Believing that Guinness will help you get lucky. (Guinness gives you courage.)

Knowing how a Guinness should be poured and how it should be drunk.

Knowing the holy trinity of Irish mixed drinks: a cordial made with blackberry brandy and Guinness, a black velvet made with Guinness and champagne, and a black and tan made with Guinness and Bass Ale.

Knowing that one good pint
deserves another.

And another and another and another.

having a genetic excuse for all
those pints.

Drinking Murphy's if your people
are from Cork.

Drinking Harp if you don't
want Guinness.

Drinking Killian's only if you're a yuppie.

Being able to curse someone out
and having it sound like poetry.

Being able to curse someone out
without their understanding what
you're saying—but they know
they were cursed.

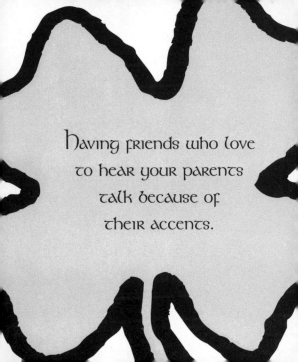

Having friends who love
to hear your parents
talk because of
their accents.

Growing up listening to your mother's John McCormack, Larry Cunningham, and Rosemary Clooney records.

Watching Frank Patterson sing on PBS specials.

Buying the videotapes of the Irish Tenors' PBS specials.

Listening to tapes of comedians Hal Roach and Niall Toibin in the car with your great-uncle Jimmy who laughs till he cries and you can't understand a word that was said.

Watching your nieces do the
Irish jig at family parties.

Seeing *Riverdance* for the first time
on a PBS special.

Seeing *Riverdance* for the
twenty-seventh time on a PBS special.

Thinking that *Riverdance* and
Lord of the Dance were the same thing.

Being embarrassed to find out that
Michael Flatley is from Chicago.

Wondering if Michael Flatley really
thinks he's the Lord.

Laughing out loud at Mike Myers's
imitation of Michael Flatley.

And still liking it when you watch
your nieces doing the Irish jig
at family parties.

Speaking of nieces: freckles.

And red hair.

Richard Daley, Tip O'Neill,
and all the Kennedys.

○

Dual citizenship.

Growing up with the Irish-American papers arriving in the mail every week.

Being more conversant in Irish politics than in American ones.

The Troubles.

Knowing who Bertie Ahern, Mary McAleese, Seamus Mallon, Ian Paisley, David Trimble, and Gerry Adams are.

Remembering the Easter Uprising.

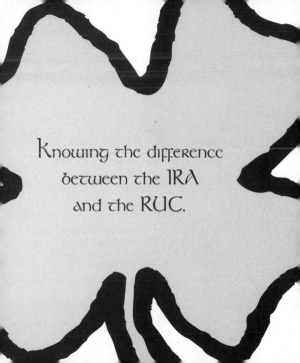

Claiming kinship with great freedom fighters like Michael Collins.

And Audie Murphy.

Being able to recite all of the
Original Twenty-six.

Galway, Leitrim, Mayo, Roscommon,
Sligo, Carlow, Dublin, Kildare, Kilkenny,
Laoighis, Longford, Louth, Meath,
Offaly, Westmeath, Wexford, Wicklow,
Clare, Cork, Kerry, Limerick, Tipperary,
Waterford, Cavan, Donegal, Monaghan.

Being able to recite the Six.

Antrim, Armagh, Down,
Fermanagh, Derry, Tyrone.

Taking pride in great Irish cities like
Chicago, Boston, and New York.

Vacations home to visit the
Ring of Kerry.

And the Giant's Causeway, the Glens of Antrim, the Aran Islands, the Mourne Mountains, the Wicklow Mountains, the Shannon River, Donegal Bay, and the Dingle Peninsula.

And knowing all these places even if you've never been because of all the old Irish songs about them.

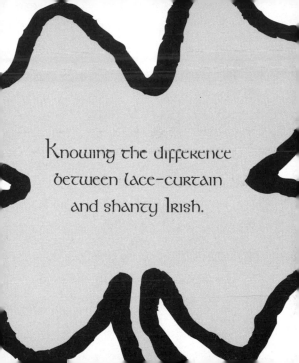

Knowing the difference between lace-curtain and shanty Irish.

having only two things hang on
the wall at home besides Irish curtains:
a portrait of JFK and a portrait
of the pope.

Not having to worry about what to
wear to grammar school.

Catholic-school skirts and kneesocks.

Navy blazers and neckties.

Wooden rulers.

Surviving the nuns.

Getting out of class to serve as an altar boy–and getting tips.

Skipping mass and going down
to the bar to watch a live broadcast
of the All-Ireland.

Skipping mass because you had
too much of the brown stuff
the night before.

Being a good Catholic and nonetheless taking the Lord's name in vain without flinching, courtesy Bejesus! Mary, Mother of God! Jesus, Mary, and Joseph!

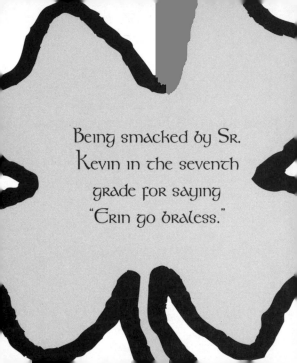

Being smacked by Sr.
Kevin in the seventh
grade for saying
"Erin go braless."

Having the clergy as a
viable career option.

Colorful expressions such as
"in me arse" in place of the
shorter and more family-acceptable
translation, "no."

A whole range of curses
not printable here.

Remembering your father pointing to a toadstool in the backyard one morning and saying, "Ah, the fairies musta had a meetin' last night."

Superstitions.

Kissing the Blarney Stone and
getting the gift of gab.

Remembering your father saying that he wished Auntie Annie had never kissed the Blarney Stone, because she already had the gift of gab.

On the other hand, your reluctance to emote true feelings can allow you to have the appearance of brooding intensity.

Feeling perpetually young since everyone in your family called you by a diminutive of your name: Paddy, Patty, Maggie, Mikey, Molly, Jimmy, Franky, Chrissie, Billy, Bridie, Terry, Tommy, Franny, Collie.

Notre Dame.

Spending fall Saturday afternoons in a blue and gold sweatshirt.

Thinking that Touchdown Jesus was the American equivalent of St. Peter's.

Respecting Regis because he went to
Notre Dame.

Being terribly depressed when rejected
by Notre Dame.

Secretly hating Domers from then on.

Wanting to go to Trinity College for junior year abroad.

The Celtics.

Great Irish entertainers like John
Wayne, Bing Crosby, Martin Sheen,
Dermot Mulroney, Dylan McDermott,
Gabriel Byrne, Aidan Quinn,
plenty of clergy, Pat O'Brien, and
Barry Fitzgerald as the priest.

The Quiet Man, The Crying Game,
The Informer, The Van,
The Commitments, The Boxer,
The Field, Waking Ned Devine,
Angela's Ashes.

Depression isn't an illness;
it's a national trait.

Music that has more to it
than just the pipes and a fiddle.

Sinead O'Connor, the Black 47, the Pogues, the Black Crows, the Smith, the Cranberries, the Corrs.

U-2 and Van Morrison.

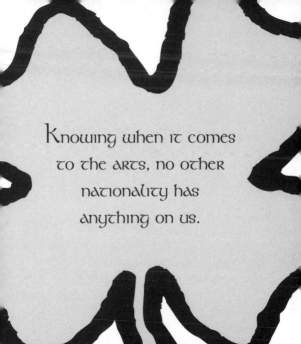

Knowing when it comes to the arts, no other nationality has anything on us.

Belonging to a long line of storytellers.

Poets like Seamus Heaney.

Writers like James Joyce.

And William Butler Yeats, Sean O'Casey, Brendan Behan, Oscar Wilde, George Bernard Shaw, Samuel Beckett, Liam O'Flaherty, and Frank O'Connor.

And Edna O'Brien, Nuala O'Faolain,
J. P. Donleavy, William Trevor,
Roddy Doyle.

Also: Frank O'Hara, Mary McCarthy,
Mary Higgins Clark, and the Hamill
brothers—and let's not forget the
McCourts: Frank, Malachy, Alfie, and
anyone else with that last name.

Hearing the legendary tales of Finn MacCool and Cú Chulainn— long before you read *Angela's Ashes*.

Knowing that you, too,
are predisposed to being
a great writer.

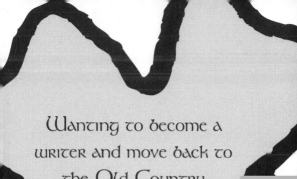

Wanting to become a
writer and move back to
the Old Country
because writers don't
have to pay taxes there.

Returning home to the Old Sod for vacation whether or not you're a writer.

Refusing to fly to Ireland on any airline but Aer Lingus.

Going to Ireland for the first time on a Brendan or CIE bus tour.

Once you get to the Old Sod, telling people "I'm Irish," even if it's only 10 percent.

Giving a detailed description of where all your Irish relatives are from and watching the natives roll their eyes like they've heard this routine one hundred times over.

Knowing that when an Irishman asks you where you're from, you're to answer with your county name and then be prepared for a smart-aleck remark about your character.

Returning back to the States with Aran sweaters for everyone in the family—which no one will ever wear because they'd sweat to death in American central heating.

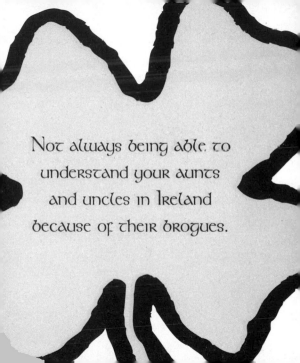

Not always being able to
understand your aunts
and uncles in Ireland
because of their brogues.

Knowing the moral of the story when they tell you about the trouble Uncle Frankie ran into with the turf accountant, even though you weren't able to understand everything that was said.

Letting them call you the Yank.

Thatched cottages.

Open hearth fires.

Understanding that when asked by a Dubliner, "How's the craic?" He's talking about conversation and fun, not street drugs.

Knowin' where the craic is mighty.

Sheep. Cows. Pubs.

Knowing how to get into the pub during the closing hours.

Having a stool in the pub that's known as yours.

Having the bartender know your drink, which he starts pouring as soon as you walk in the door.

Golf.

Feeling that you have an innate ability
to play links courses.

Bluffing to your buddies that you shot par on Ballybunnion.

Routing for Darren Clarke, Christy O'Connor, and Padraig Harrington in the British Opens.

Connemara ponies.

Gaelic football.

The All-Ireland.

Rooting for your home county,
even if it's really your grandfather's
home county.

Getting stuck in traffic at milking time.

While driving the Ring of Kerry,
getting stuck behind a farmer in
his 1972 Mercedes with three sheep
in the backseat.

Getting stuck while driving the
Ring of Kerry because the sheep—
the ones not in the farmer's backseat—
won't get out of the road.

Being born with a foolproof radar
for finding a fine pub in a
strange town.

Knowing you don't have to go to Ireland to find an Irish bar—every town in America has one.

Learning at an early age that the
bartender is your best friend.

Living by the Irish economic code:
Big tips mean free rounds.

A natural-born ability
to consume large quantities
of ale at Irish bars.

Stupid pub songs.

Reading the Irish social pages,
aka the obituaries.

Knowing that the obituaries serve
as a map to free drinks
all over town.

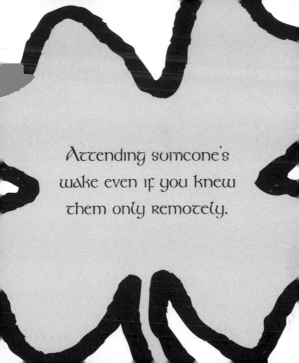

Attending sumeone's
wake even if you knew
them only remotely.

Lace curtains.

Lace doilies.

Carrickmacross lace.

Lace-curtain Irish.

Shanty Irish.

Hearing your mother's family call your
father's family shanty Irish.

Hearing your father's family call
your mother's family tinkers.

Wondering what will become of you
if you're half shanty and half tinker.

Not flinching when your mother
threatens, "I'll brain ya!"

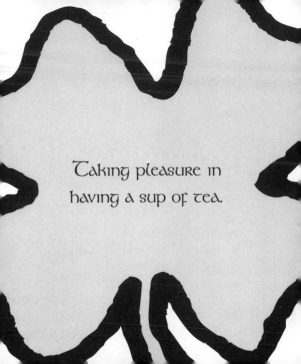

Taking pleasure in
having a sup of tea.

Putting on the kettle.

Letting the tea draw.

Tea with milk.

Tea with sugar.

Tea with milk and sugar.

Milk and sugar with tea.

Tea with honey.

Tea with milk and honey.

Milk and honey with tea.

Grandad insisting that he'd
only own an Irish dog.

Border collies, greyhounds,
Kerry blues, Irish wolfhounds,
cocker spaniels, Irish setters.

Being wary of Italians.

Disliking the English.

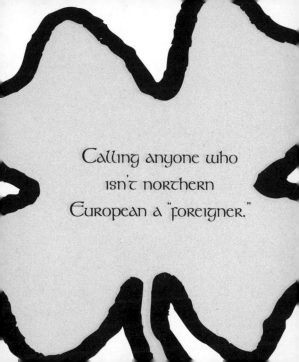

Calling anyone who
isn't northern
European a "foreigner."

To-the-point blessings like:

"May those who love us, love us;
and those who don't love us,
may God turn their hearts.
And if He doesn't turn their hearts,
may He turn their ankles
so we know them by their limps!"

Or, more important, this one:

"May the road rise up to meet you,
and the wind be forever at your back,
and may you be in heaven a half hour
before the devil knows you're dead."

Knowing to start leaving a party an hour before you truly intend to leave because of Irish good-byes.